DATE DUE			

Designed and produced by
Aladdin Books Ltd
70 Old Compton Street
LONDON W1

First published in the
United States in 1988 by
Gloucester Press
387 Park Avenue South
New York NY 10016

ISBN 0 531 17124 8

Library of Congress Catalog
Card Number: 88-50500

Certain illustrations originally published in
The Closer Look Series

Whales

Contents

The biggest animal in the world   7

Getting along   8

Sea mammals   10

Baleen whales   12

Right whales   14

The Rorqual family   16

Whale babies   18

Toothed whales   20

Dolphins   22

Intelligent mammals   24

Killer whales   26

Saving the whale   28

Index   29

Whales

Kate Petty

Illustrated by
Norman Weaver

small world

Gloucester Press

New York · London · Toronto · Sydney

Blue whale

Fin whale

Right whale

Humpback whale

Sei whale

Bryde's whale

The biggest animal in the world
This Blue whale is the same length
as three buses end to end.
It is over 90 feet long and weighs 100 tons.
Blue whales are the largest living animals.

All these whales are giants.
Compare them with the Blue whale.

Getting along

Whales move gracefully through the water
despite their enormous size. They beat
their tails up and down to propel themselves
along and use their flippers for steering.
Blue whales can move at over 20 miles per hour
but big whales are more likely to travel
at about 5 miles per hour. They are surprisingly
acrobatic.This Humpback is leaping out of the
water before diving back in again.

Humpback whale leaping out of the water

Sea mammals

Whales have the same streamlined shape as
fish for moving easily through the water.
But whales are mammals like us and produce
milk to feed their babies. They are descended
from creatures which once lived on land.

Bottlenose dolphins

The fish is scaly but the whale's skin is soft.
The fish breathes through gills but the whale
has lungs and breathes through a blowhole
on top of its head. The fish is cold-blooded
but the whale is warm-blooded.

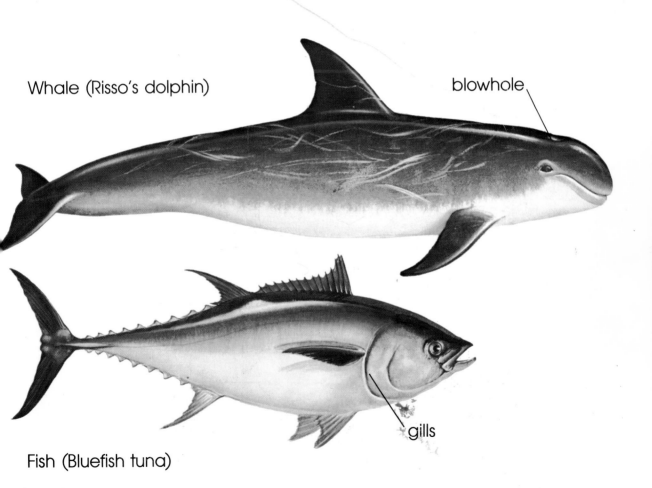

Whale (Risso's dolphin)

blowhole

gills

Fish (Bluefish tuna)

Baleen whales

There are two separate groups of whales –
toothed whales and baleen whales.
A baleen whale does not need teeth.
Instead, a fringe of bony plates
called baleen hangs down from the
roof of its mouth. When the whale
takes in a gulp of sea water
the baleen works like a net and holds
back the tiny creatures from the water.
The whale swallows them whole.

Right whale

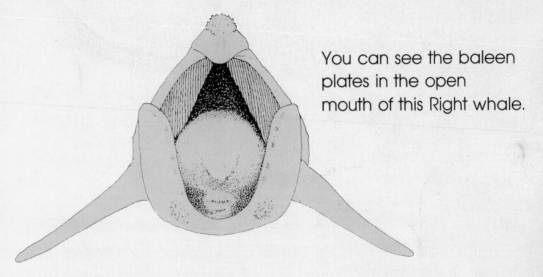

You can see the baleen
plates in the open
mouth of this Right whale.

Some of the biggest whales are baleen whales.
The Blue whale belongs to the Rorqual family.

Rorqual

Right whales

These whales were called Right whales because
they were once the "right" whales to hunt.
Right whales were easy to hunt because they
swam close to the shore and moved very slowly.

Right whales often have barnacles and "whale lice" on their skins.

The valuable plates of baleen, or "whalebone,"
were sold to make combs and corsets.
So many Right whales were killed that
they are now quite rare.

Patagonian Right whale

The Rorqual family

Rorquals were too fast-moving for the early hunters but they became victims of modern whalers with their explosive harpoons.
The Rorqual family includes some of the biggest whales, such as Blue, Fin, Sei and Bryde's.

A pod of Fin whales

Rorquals all have deep grooves down their throats and bellies, which probably help them to cool down. They are sometimes called "Finbacks" because of the fin set a long way down their backs. They live in family groups called "pods."

Whale babies

Unlike land mammals, a whale calf is born
tail first. Once the calf's head has emerged
the mother and other female whales help it
to the surface to take its first breath.
Then it is able to swim along with the others.

The calf stays close to its mother and feeds on her milk. Young whales grow very fast, doubling their birth weight in the first week. They "talk" to their parents in special whistles and squeaks as they swim along.

Humpback whales with baby

Toothed whales

Most whales, including dolphins, are toothed
whales. Dolphins have over 200 teeth. The
Sperm whale has less than 50 teeth. It feeds
on squid which it hunts a long way below the
surface. Sperm whales can dive deeper and
stay underwater longer than other whales.
They use sound waves to find their prey.

Sperm whales

A giant squid can be
over 30 feet long

Dolphins

Dolphins are the smallest whales. Most of them are less than 10 feet long. They are a slender, streamlined shape with beak-like snouts. Dolphins are sociable creatures and live in herds of about 20. During the mating season many herds join together to form huge schools of over a hundred dolphins.

A school of Common dolphins

Some of the 36 different dolphins

Common dolphin

Bottlenose dolphin

White-sided dolphin

Commerson's dolphin

Hourglass dolphin

Intelligent mammals

There are many stories about dolphins helping
swimmers in trouble. This could be
because dolphins help one another if they
are in distress. But dolphins are naturally
friendly and curious. A female dolphin called
"Opo" made friends with bathers in New Zealand
and sometimes gave short rides to children.

lphins kept in oceanariums seem
enjoy learning all sorts of tricks.
en Killer whales, the largest dolphins,
e gentle and playful when kept
captivity.

Pilot whale jumping for fish

forming Pacific dolphins

Killer whales

Killer whales are the wolves of the
polar seas. They hunt in large packs,
working as a team. They kill mammals as
well as fish. A pack of them can tackle
even the biggest whales.

Killer whales come up out of the water
to look for seals or penguins on the ice.
They smash the ice from underneath
and knock their prey into the water.

Killer whales

Saving the whale

Whales are intelligent, feeling mammals.
Their bodies were once valuable for many
things that have been replaced by
modern plastics and oils. Now whales are
killed mostly for meat to be served in
expensive restaurants. Many people feel that
whaling should be stopped before these
magnificent animals disappear altogether.

Index

baleen 12, 13, 15
Blue whale 6, 7, 16
Bottlenose dolphin 10, 23
breathing 11
Bryde's whale 6, 16

calves 18, 19
Commerson's dolphin 23
Common dolphin 23

dolphins 20, 22-23, 24-25

Fin whale 6, 16

Hourglass dolphin 23
Humpback whale 6, 8, 9, 18

Killer whale 25, 26-27

Pacific dolphin 25
Pilot whale 25

Right whale 6, 13, 14, 15
Risso's dolphin 11
Rorquals 13, 16, 17

Sei whale 6, 16
Sperm whale 20
squid 21

White-sided dolphin 23

PRINTED IN BELGIUM BY proost INTERNATIONAL BOOK PRODUCTION

Dad